I0975994

Presented to

_____

by_____

on_____

Are Angels Real?

Kathleen Long Bostrom
Illustrated by Elena Kucharik

Tyndale House Publishers, Inc.
WHEATON, ILLINOIS

Visit Tyndale's exciting Web site at www.tyndale.com

Edited by Betty Free
Designed by Catherine Bergstrom

Scripture quotations are taken from the *Holy Bible*, New Living Translation, copyright
© 1996. Used by permission of Tyndale House Publishers, Inc., Wheaton, Illinois 60189.
All rights reserved.

Library of Congress Cataloging-in-Publication Data

Bostrom, Kathleen Long.
    Are angels real? / Kathleen Long Bostrom; illustrated by Elena Kucharik.
        p. cm.
    ISBN 0-8423-3959-0 (hc)
    1. Angels—Juvenile literature. [1. Angels.] I. Kucharik, Elena, ill. II. Title.
BT966.2 .B63 2001
235'.3—dc21   00-059916

Printed in Italy

07 06 05 04 03 02
8   7   6

To Greg, my husband,
who believed I could do this before all the rest;
To Betty, my editor,
whose work with my words helps to bring out my best;
To the glory of God—
to serve you with honor is ever my quest.

I've heard there are angels.

Oh, can it be true?

Are angels for real?

And just what do they do?

Do I have an angel

that looks after me?

Can I talk to angels?

Can they hear and see?

5

Will angels be glad

if I do what is right?

Does God tuck them into

their cloud beds at night?

Do angels wear slippers

or sandals or shoes?

I know I'd go barefoot

if I got to choose!

Do angels have power?

Are they very strong?

If I am afraid,

will they sing me a song?

Do angels have wings,

and can all of them fly?

Do angels grow older,

and then do they die?

Are there many angels,

or only a few?

When I go to heaven,

can I be one too?

Are angels for real?

    There is no need to guess.

The Bible assures us

    the answer is yes!

So, who made the angels?

    Well, God did, that's who!

And God gives the angels

    Their own jobs to do.

23

When God has a message,

he often will use

An angel to bring us

the wonderful news.

The angels serve God

in their own special ways

26

And then give to God

all the glory and praise.

You can't always see them,

but this you should know:

The angels are with you

wherever you go.

Yet when you have something

important to say,

It's God, not the angels,

to whom you should pray.

Tell God that you're sorry

for doing what's wrong.

Then all of the angels

will sing a glad song!

33

Elena

Angels are spirits—

they don't need to sleep.

God never says, "Quiet!

Now don't make a peep!"

As far as what angels

   might wear for their clothes,

They dress up in light

   from their head to their toes!

Their power is used

to obey God's commands.

They even can hold back

the wind with their hands!

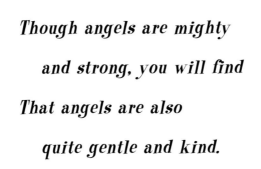

Though angels are mighty

and strong, you will find

That angels are also

quite gentle and kind.

41

When you are afraid,

here is what you can do:

Imagine that angels

are singing to you.

Angels are speedy,

and this is no lie—

They move place to place

in the blink of an eye.

Now, here is another
remarkable thing:
All angels can fly,
but they don't all need wings!

There may be some angels

with no wings, it's true,

While some may have six,

and still others have two.

Angels aren't born,

    and they never grow old.

They never get married,

    from what we are told.

Angels don't die,

    though that seems rather odd,

For they are already

    in heaven with God.

Just how many are there?

What is the amount?

Thousands and millions—

too many to count!

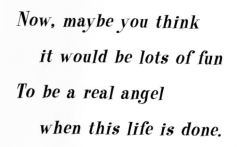

Now, maybe you think
   it would be lots of fun
To be a real angel
   when this life is done.

We won't become angels,
   but that is OK.
We'll all be together
   in heaven someday.

Until that time comes,

here's a word of advice:

Treat everyone kindly,
and try to be nice.

If you share God's love
as we're all meant to do,
You just might be helping
an angel out too!

Bible References

Here are some Bible verses to talk about as you read this book again with your child. You may want to open your Bible as you read the verses. This will help your little one understand that the answers in this poem come from God's Word, the Bible.

Are angels for real? There is no need to guess.
The Bible assures us the answer is yes!
So, who made the angels? Well, God did, that's who!
And God gives the angels their own jobs to do.

Christ is the one through whom God created everything in heaven and earth. He made the things we can see and the things we can't see. COLOSSIANS 1:16

Praise the Lord, you angels of his, you mighty creatures who carry out his plans, listening for each of his commands. Yes, praise the Lord, you armies of angels who serve him and do his will! PSALM 103:20-21

When God has a message, he often will use
An angel to bring us the wonderful news.

> The angel said [to Zechariah], "I am Gabriel! I stand in the very presence of God. It was he who sent me to bring you this good news!" LUKE 1:19

> God sent the angel Gabriel to Nazareth. . . . "[Mary,] God has decided to bless you!" LUKE 1:26, 30

> An angel of the Lord appeared among [the shepherds]. . . . "I bring you good news of great joy for everyone!" LUKE 2:9-10

The angels serve God in their own special ways
And then give to God all the glory and praise.

> In a great chorus they sang, "Holy, holy, holy is the Lord Almighty! The whole earth is filled with his glory!" The glorious singing shook the Temple to its foundations, and the entire sanctuary was filled with smoke. ISAIAH 6:3-4

> When he presented his honored Son to the world, God said, "Let all the angels of God worship him." HEBREWS 1:6

**You can't always see them, but this you should know:
The angels are with you wherever you go.**

He orders his angels to protect you wherever you go. They will hold you with their hands to keep you from striking your foot on a stone. PSALM 91:11-12

Gabriel roused me with a touch and helped me to my feet. DANIEL 8:18

An angel of the Lord came at night, opened the gates of the jail, and brought [the apostles] out. ACTS 5:19

**Yet when you have something important to say,
It's God, not the angels, to whom you should pray.**

Don't let anyone say you must worship angels, even though they say they have had visions about this. COLOSSIANS 2:18

The angel said to me, . . ."These are true words that come from God."Then I fell down at his feet to worship him, but he said, "No, don't worship me. For I am a servant of God, just like you and other believers who testify of their faith in Jesus. Worship God." REVELATION 19:9-10

**Tell God that you're sorry for doing what's wrong.
Then all of the angels will sing a glad song!**

There is joy in the presence of God's angels when even one sinner repents. LUKE 15:10

**Angels are spirits—they don't need to sleep.
God never says, "Quiet! Now don't make a peep!"**

As [Jacob] slept, he dreamed of a stairway that reached from earth to heaven. And he saw the angels of God going up and down on it. GENESIS 28:12

Last night an angel of the God to whom I belong and whom I serve stood beside me, and he said, "Don't be afraid, Paul." ACTS 27:23-24

Angels are only servants. They are spirits sent from God to care for those who will receive salvation. HEBREWS 1:14

As far as what angels might wear for their clothes,
They dress up in light from their head to their toes!

Suddenly there was a great earthquake, because an angel of the Lord came down from heaven and rolled aside the stone and sat on it. His face shone like lightning, and his clothing was as white as snow. MATTHEW 28:2-3

Suddenly, there was a bright light in the cell, and an angel of the Lord stood before Peter. ACTS 12:7

Then I saw another mighty angel coming down from heaven, surrounded by a cloud, with a rainbow over his head. His face shone like the sun, and his feet were like pillars of fire. REVELATION 10:1

**Their power is used to obey God's commands.
They even can hold back the wind with their hands!**

Then I saw four angels standing at the four corners of the earth, holding back the four winds from blowing upon the earth. REVELATION 7:1

After all this I saw another angel come down from heaven with great authority, and the earth grew bright with his splendor. REVELATION 18:1

**Though angels are mighty and strong, you will find
That angels are also quite gentle and kind.**

[Elijah] lay down and slept under the broom tree. But as he was sleeping, an angel touched him and told him, "Get up and eat!" . . . Then the angel of the Lord came again and touched him and said, "Get up and eat some more, for there is a long journey ahead of you." I KINGS 19:5, 7

If a special messenger from heaven is there to intercede for a person, to declare that he is upright, God will be gracious and say, "Set him free." JOB 33:23-24

**When you are afraid, here is what you can do:
Imagine that angels are singing to you.**

[The shepherds] were terribly frightened, but the angel reassured them. "Don't be afraid!" he said. "I bring you good news of great joy for everyone! . . ." Suddenly, the angel was joined by a vast host of others—the armies of heaven—praising God: "Glory to God in the highest heaven, and peace on earth to all whom God favors."
LUKE 2:9-10, 13-14

The angel spoke to the women [at the tomb]. "Don't be afraid!" he said. "I know you are looking for Jesus, who was crucified. He isn't here! He has been raised from the dead, just as he said would happen." MATTHEW 28:5-6

Angels are speedy, and this is no lie—
They move place to place in the blink of an eye.

God calls his angels "messengers swift as the wind, and servants made of flaming fire." HEBREWS 1:7

I saw another angel flying through the heavens, carrying the everlasting Good News to preach to the people who belong to this world—to every nation, tribe, language, and people. REVELATION 14:6

Now, here is another remarkable thing:
All angels can fly, but they don't all need wings!
There may be some angels with no wings, it's true,
While some may have six, and still others have two.

[An angel appeared as a man to Samson's parents before their baby was born:] Manoah ran back with his wife and asked, "Are you the man who talked to my wife?" . . . Manoah finally realized it was the angel of the Lord. JUDGES 13:11, 21

[Isaiah saw angels called seraphim:] Hovering around [the Lord] were mighty seraphim, each with six wings. ISAIAH 6:2

[Ezekiel saw angels called cherubim:] The moving wings of the cherubim sounded like the voice of God Almighty. EZEKIEL 10:5

[Gold cherubim were placed in Solomon's Temple:]
Solomon made two figures shaped like cherubim
and overlaid them with gold. . . . One wing of the
first figure . . . touched the Temple wall. The other
wing . . . touched one of the wings of the
second figure. 2 CHRONICLES 3:10-11

Angels aren't born, and they never grow old.
They never get married, from what we are told.
Angels don't die, though that seems rather odd,
For they are already in heaven with God.

Praise him, all his angels! Praise him, all the armies of
heaven! PSALM 148:2

Jesus replied, ". . . When the dead rise, they won't be
married. They will be like the angels in heaven."
MARK 12:24–25

Just how many are there? What is the amount?
Thousands and millions—too many to count!

> I looked again, and I heard the singing of thousands and millions of angels around the throne and the living beings and the elders. REVELATION 5:11

Now, maybe you think it would be lots of fun
To be a real angel when this life is done.
We won't become angels, but that is OK.
We'll all be together in heaven someday.

> He will send forth his angels to gather together his chosen ones from all over the world—from the farthest ends of the earth and heaven. MARK 13:27

> You have come to Mount Zion, to the city of the living God, the heavenly Jerusalem, and to thousands of angels in joyful assembly. HEBREWS 12:22

Until that time comes, here's a word of advice:
Treat everyone kindly, and try to be nice.
If you share God's love as we're all meant to do,
You just might be helping an angel out too!

Don't forget to show hospitality to strangers, for some
who have done this have entertained angels without
realizing it! HEBREWS 13:2

About the Author

Kathleen Long Bostrom is the author of seven Little Blessings books. Two are board books, and five have poetic questions based on actual questions from "little blessings" she has known. She has also written another book of verse, *The World that God Made*, plus numerous newspaper and magazine articles, and several prize-winning sermons.

Kathy earned a doctor of ministry in preaching degree from McCormick Theological Seminary in Chicago, Illinois, and a master of arts in Christian education and master of divinity degree from Princeton Theological Seminary. She also has a bachelor of arts degree in psychology from California State University, Long Beach, California.

Kathy and her husband, Greg, live with their three children—Christopher, Amy, and David—in Wildwood, Illinois. Kathy and Greg serve as co-pastors of Wildwood Presbyterian Church.

Kathy hopes that her books will be used not only with parents and children but in Sunday school classes, preschools, and church worship settings.

About the Illustrator

Elena Kucharik, well-known Care Bears artist, has created the Little Blessings characters. They appear in a line of Little Blessings products for young children and their families.

Born in Cleveland, Ohio, Elena received a bachelor of fine arts degree in commercial art at Kent State University. After graduation she worked as a greeting card artist and art director at American Greetings Corporation in Cleveland.

For the past 25 years Elena has been a freelance illustrator. During this time she was the lead artist and developer of Care Bears, as well as a designer and illustrator for major corporations and publishers. For the past 10 years Elena has been focusing her talents on illustrations for children's books.

Elena and her husband live in New Canaan, Connecticut, and have two grown daughters.

Other products in the Little Blessings line

Bible for Little Hearts
Prayers for Little Hearts
Promises for Little Hearts
Lullabies for Little Hearts
Lullabies Cassette
Lullabies CD

What Is God Like?
Who Is Jesus?
What about Heaven?
What Is Prayer?

Blessings Everywhere
Rain or Shine
God Makes Nighttime Too
Birthday Blessings
Christmas Blessings
God Loves You

Little Blessings New Testament
*   & Psalms*